TREASURE ISLAND

The *Oxford Progressive English Readers* series provides a wide range of reading for learners of English.

Each book in the series has been written to follow the strict guidelines of a syllabus, wordlist and structure list. The texts are graded according to these guidelines; Grade 1 at a 1,400 word level, Grade 2 at a 2,100 word level, Grade 3 at a 3,100 word level, Grade 4 at a 3,700 word level and Grade 5 at a 5,000 word level.

The latest methods of text analysis, using specially designed software, ensure that readability is carefully controlled at every level. Any new words which are vital to the mood and style of the story are explained within the text, and reoccur throughout for maximum reinforcement. New language items are also clarified by attractive illustrations.

Each book has a short section containing carefully graded exercises and controlled activities, which test both global and specific understanding.

Treasure Island

Robert Louis Stevenson

Hong Kong
Oxford University Press
Oxford Singapore Tokyo

Oxford University Press

Oxford   New York   Toronto
Kuala Lumpur   Singapore   Hong Kong   Tokyo
Delhi   Bombay   Calcutta   Madras   Karachi
Nairobi   Dar es Salaam   Cape Town
Melbourne   Auckland   Madrid

and associated companies in
Berlin   Ibadan

Oxford is a trade mark of Oxford University Press

First published 1992
Fourth impression 1994

© Oxford University Press 1992

Illustrated by K.Y. Chan

Syllabus designer: David Foulds

Text processing and analysis by Luxfield Consultants Ltd.

ISBN 0 19 585273 7

Printed in Hong Kong
Published by Oxford University Press (Hong Kong) Ltd
18/F Warwick House, Taikoo Place, 979 King's Road,
Quarry Bay, Hong Kong

CONTENTS

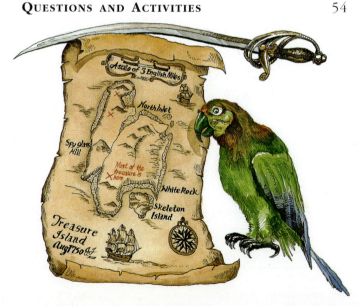

1

THE ADMIRAL BENBOW INN

The Captain

My name is Jim Hawkins. When I was a boy I lived with my mother and father in an inn called the Admiral Benbow. My father was the owner of the inn. One day, an old seaman *5* came to stay with us. I remember him well.

He was a tall, strong man.
On his face was a mark,
from a sword cut. He brought his sea chest with him. *10*
This was a large wooden box. He kept it locked all the time. We called this rough old man 'the Captain'.

One morning the Captain spoke to me. He said he wanted me to watch for a seaman with one leg. As soon as I saw this man I had to tell the Captain. If I *15* did this he would give me a silver coin every month.

In the winter a man did come. But not the man with a wooden leg.

This man looked very rough. He had only three fingers on his left hand. He carried a knife. I asked *20* him what he wanted to drink. He said, 'Rum.'

Black Dog

I brought him some rum, and then he said, 'There is
a man called "the Captain" staying here. I think he is
my friend, Bill. Tell me, boy, is the Captain a tall, old
5   man, with a cut on his face?'

'Yes,' I said.

'Then he is Bill. Old Billy Bones. Is he in the house
now?'

I told him that the Captain was out.

10   'Where?' he said. I pointed to the sea.

The inn door was open. We heard someone
coming. The stranger waited behind the door. He
pulled me behind it with him. He took out his sword.
I thought he was going to kill me with it. I was afraid.

15   The Captain came in. He walked across the room
to his breakfast. He did not see us.

'Bill,' said the stranger.

Then the Captain saw us. His face went white. He
suddenly looked old and ill.

20   'Black Dog!' said the Captain. 'What do you want?'

'I will have a glass of rum. Then we'll sit and talk
like old friends,' said the stranger.

I brought them their rum, and went out of the
room.

25   ## The fight

Suddenly, there was shouting and other noises. The
chair and the table fell over. Then I heard a cry of
pain. I saw Black Dog run away. On Black Dog's left
arm there was a lot of blood.

30   'Jim,' the Captain said, 'bring me rum.' He looked
very weak.

'Are you hurt?' I asked.

'Rum,' he said again. 'I must go away from here. Rum, rum.'

I ran out to find the rum. Then I heard a loud fall. I ran back and found the Captain on the floor.   5
My mother also heard the noise, and she ran downstairs to help me. His face was a terrible colour.

Doctor Livesey was at the inn. He had come to visit my father who was very ill. 'Oh, doctor,' we said, 'what shall we do? Where is the Captain hurt?'

'Hurt!' said the doctor, 'He is not hurt. He just drinks too much rum. He's drunk!' The Captain tried   15
to sit up. 'Where is Black Dog?' he shouted.

'There is no Black Dog here,' said the doctor. 'You have been drinking rum. Come, now, try to walk. I will help you to your bed.'

The black mark   20

At twelve o'clock I went to the Captain's room. I took him a cold drink and some medicine. He was on his bed. He looked weak, but excited.

'Did that doctor say how long I must stay in bed?' he asked.   25

'One week,' I said.

'No,' he shouted, 'a week! I can't do that. They will soon give me the black mark. Did you see that seaman today, Jim?'

'Black Dog?' I asked.

5 'Yes, Black Dog,' he said. 'He is bad but the seamen with him are worse. We all worked on the same ship once. Flint was the captain. I was the first mate. I was Flint's friend.

'They want my old wooden box. If they give me 10 the black mark before I can go away, then you must go to that doctor. Tell him to bring many men here. They will have to fight those seamen.'

'What is the black mark, Captain?' I asked.

'It means something bad will happen, Jim.'

15 **The blind beggar**

Soon after that my father died. A few days later, at three o'clock in the afternoon, I was standing at the inn door. I was thinking about my father.

I saw someone coming slowly along the road. He 20 was blind. He used a stick to help him find his way. He looked old and weak. He wore a big, old coat. He was ugly. He called out, 'Will any friend tell a poor blind man where he is?'

'You are at the Admiral Benbow inn,' I said.

25 'I hear a voice, a young voice,' he said. 'Will you give me your hand and lead me in?'

I gave my hand to this terrible blind person.

He held my hand very hard. I was afraid and tried to pull away. The blind man looked weak, but he 30 was very strong. He pulled me closer.

'Now, boy,' he said, 'take me to Billy Bones, or I'll break your arm.' I was very afraid. We went into the living room. I knew the Captain was sitting there, drinking rum. The blind man held me close to him with his strong arm.

The Captain dies

The poor Captain looked round and saw us. He looked frightened. He tried to stand up.

'Bill,' said the blind beggar, 'I can't see you, but I can hear everything. Give me your right hand.'

I saw the blind man put something into the Captain's hand.

'And now that is done,' said the blind man. He went out of the inn. He moved quickly. I could hear the tap, tap, tapping of his stick. The Captain and I did not move for a few seconds. He opened his hand. He looked at what the blind man had given him. Then he stood up quickly. He put his hand on his throat. He made a strange noise, and then fell on the floor.

I called my mother and ran to the Captain, but he was dead.

THE WOODEN BOX

The Captain's chest

Mother came in. We were both very afraid. I knelt
down. On the floor, close to the Captain's hand, there
was a piece of paper. It was black on one side. I
5 knew that this was the black mark. On the paper
were these words: 'Ten o'clock, tonight.' 'The Captain
had until ten o'clock,
mother,' I said. 'It is
just six o'clock now.'
10 The Captain never
paid for his room. My
mother wanted to see
if he had any money
in the old wooden
15 box.We found the
key, then we went
upstairs to his little
bedroom. The chest
was still there. My mother opened it.

20 At the bottom of the chest we found a cloth bag.
Inside were papers, and some gold coins.
Mother began counting the money. We had
counted half the money when I heard a noise. The
blind man was coming back. He hit the inn door with
25 his stick. He tried to open it, but it was locked. Then
it was quiet for a long time. A few minutes later we
heard the tapping of his stick again. He was walking
away.

Then we heard the noise of people coming down the hill. My mother was very frightened. We knew we had to run.

'I'll take this money,' mother said, jumping up.

'And I'll take this,' I said. I picked up the papers 5 in the cloth bag.

We went downstairs, opened the door and began to run.

Thieves

I wanted to know what was happening. I hid behind 10 a small tree, and from there I could see the inn.

Seven or eight men were running towards the inn.The blind man was coming along behind them.

'Break open the door,' he shouted.

Some of them went into the house. Two men 15 stayed on the road with the beggar. A voice called from the room upstairs.

'Pew, they were here before us. Someone has opened the chest.'

'Is it there?' the blind man, Pew, shouted. 20

'Some money is here,' said the man.

'I don't want the money, I want that map.'

'We can't find it.'

Then Pew called to the man downstairs, 'Has Bill got it in his pockets?' 25

'No, there is nothing here.'

'The people who own the inn must have it. That boy, he has taken everything,' said Pew. 'Look for them. Find them.'

Suddenly there was the sound of someone calling 30 from the hill. Then I heard horses. The seamen came out and began to run away.

In half a minute only one man was left. It was Pew. He walked along the road, tapping his stick and calling to his friends. He shouted and ran when he heard the horses, but he fell down. Quickly, he got up again, but he was not fast enough. A horse ran over him.

The men on the horses stopped because of Pew. Pew was dead. 'I must go and tell Dr Livesey about this,' one of the men said.

'Can I come?' I asked. I wanted to show the doctor the papers I had taken from the Captain's wooden box.

At Squire Trelawney's house

We rode quickly all the way. Dr Livesey was not at home. He had gone to visit Squire Trelawney, so we went to the squire's house.

When we arrived, one of the squire's servants led us through a long hall. We went into a big room with a lot of books in it. Dr Livesey and the squire were sitting there by the fire.

The squire was a big man. He had an honest face.

'Come in, Mr Dance,' the squire said to the man.

'Good evening, Mr Dance,' said the doctor. 'And good evening to you, Jim, my friend. Good to see you.'

Mr Dance told the squire and the doctor his story. The two gentlemen listened and looked at each other. They were surprised and interested.

'Mr Dance,' said the squire. 'You are a very brave man. And you are a brave boy, too, Jim.'

Mr Dance left. The doctor said to me, 'Jim, do you have the papers they were looking for?'

'Here they are, sir,' I said. I gave him the cloth bag.

'Do you know who Flint was?' asked the doctor.

'Of course,' said the squire. 'He and his seamen were very evil men. They attacked many ships. They killed many people and stole much treasure. Flint was the worst pirate ever.' 5

'So you think he had some money, then?' the doctor asked.

'Money,' shouted the squire, 'Of course he did. All pirates have money.' 10

'Well,' said the doctor, 'this cloth bag has something important in it. It will tell us where to find Flint's money.'

The Captain's papers

The doctor opened the bag. He found a large piece 15 of paper inside. It was a map of an island. Everything was marked on it.

The names of the hills and the harbours. The island was nine miles long, and five miles wide. There were two good harbours and a hill in the centre called 'Spy-glass Hill'. The most important things were three red crosses. Two of them were on the north of the island. The other one was in the south-west. Beside it someone had written in red ink: 'Most of the treasure is here.'

'Livesey,' said the squire. 'We must look for this treasure. Tomorrow I will go to Bristol. In three weeks' time we will have the best ship in England and the best sailors, too. Jim can come. He will be cabin-boy. You, Livesey, will be the ship's doctor, and I will be the admiral. Three of my servants, Redruth, Joyce and Hunter, will come with us. It will be easy to find the treasure. And we'll all be rich.'

'Squire,' said the doctor, 'I'll go with you, and I'm sure Jim will too. But, do not tell anyone else about this. There are some bad men who know about this map. They are not far away, and they all want that money. From now on, do not speak to anyone else about the treasure.'

'Livesey,' said the squire, 'I will not say a word.'

I Go to Bristol

The *Hispaniola*

We waited many weeks. Then, one day, a letter arrived. It was to Dr Livesey and Redruth. Doctor Livesey was away in London. Redruth could not read, 5 so I opened the letter and read it for him. This is what the letter said:

> *Old Anchor Inn,*
> *Bristol, March 1,17—*
>
> *Dear Dr Livesey,* 10
> *I have bought a ship. She is in the harbour and ready to go to sea. She is a good ship, but not very large. Her name is the Hispaniola.*
> *Everyone here was most interested when I said we were going to look for treasure.* 15

'Redruth,' I said, 'the doctor will not like that. The squire has told people about the treasure.' I read more of the letter:

> *At first, no-one would join the crew of our ship. I wanted twenty sailors, to help fight* 20 *pirates. Then, one day, I was lucky. I met a man who was once a sailor, but now he has a small inn. He said he knew all the sailors in Bristol. This man helped me find twenty men. Most of them are very ugly, but they all look strong and* 25 *brave.*

The man who helped me wanted to go back to sea, too. He told me he could work as a ship's cook, so I gave him the job. His name is Long John Silver. He has only one good leg.

5   *Both of you come to Bristol quickly. Bring Jim with you.*

John Trelawney.

Long John Silver

After I read the letter I was very excited. The next
10 day, after dinner, I said goodbye to my mother. I was sad to leave the Admiral Benbow. Then Redruth and I rode to Bristol.

Squire Trelawney was staying at an inn near the harbour. As we walked to the inn we passed many
15 ships. They were from many different places.

We found Squire Trelawney. When he saw us he said, 'Good. You're here. The doctor arrived last night. We are all here now!'

'Sir,' I said, 'when do we sail?'

20 'Sail?' he said. 'We sail tomorrow.'

The next day, after breakfast, the squire gave me a note to take to Long John Silver at his inn. I found it easily.

It was a happy little place. It looked clean and new.
25 The people inside were all sailors. They talked very loudly. I stood at the door. I was afraid to go in.

I saw a man come into the room. I knew he was Long John. He had only one good leg. The other was a piece of wood. He used a crutch but he moved
30 about very quickly. He was tall and strong, and had a big, happy face. He looked kind and clever. He laughed a lot.

I walked towards him.

'Are you Mr Silver?' I asked.

'Yes, my boy,' he said, 'that is my name. Who are you?' He saw the note in my hand. 'Oh!' he said, after he had read the note, 'You are the new cabin-boy.'   5

Black Dog again

Then I saw someone move. A man stood up and ran out of the door. I knew who he was. It was the man with only three fingers on his hand. He was the one who came to the Admiral Benbow to see the Captain.   10

'Stop him!' I shouted. 'That's Black Dog.'

'Who?' Long John asked. 'Black what?'

'Black Dog, sir,' I said. 'He is a pirate.'

'A pirate?' said Silver. 'And in my inn? Well I don't like that.' He called to one of the sailors, 'Ben, Ben.   15 Run and catch him, quickly!' Then he looked at me. 'A pirate, you say, Jim? Black Dog? No, I don't know that name. But I think I have seen him before.

Oh yes, I remember now, he often came in here with a blind beggar.'

'I knew the blind man, too,' I said. 'His name was Pew.'

5 'It was,' shouted Silver. He was excited. 'Pew! That was his name. He looked very bad. If we can catch Black Dog, Squire Trelawney will be very pleased.'

I watched John Silver very carefully. I had seen Black Dog in his inn. And I did not know if Silver 10 was an honest man. But he was a clever man. Ben came back and said he could not find Black Dog. Silver was angry. 'Jim,' he said, 'we must go and tell Squire Trelawney about this.'

The squire is told

15 Silver and I walked back along the harbour together. He told me about the different ships we passed. He knew many interesting things about ships and the sea. I enjoyed listening to him. I thought that I was very lucky to be sailing with Long John Silver.

20 When we arrived at the inn, Dr Livesey and the squire were sitting together drinking.

Long John told them the story. The two gentlemen were sorry that Black Dog had escaped. They thanked Long John for trying to help. Then Long John 25 took his crutch and went out of the door.

'Everyone must be on the ship at four this afternoon,' the squire shouted to him.

'Yes,' said Long John.

'Squire,' said Dr Livesey. 'I think Long John is a 30 good man.'

'Yes, he is a good man,' said the squire. 'Now, we must go to the ship. Come on, Jim.'

GUNS AND SWORDS

Captain Smollett

The *Hispaniola* was in the middle of the harbour. We took a small boat to reach her. When we arrived I saw that the captain and the squire were not friends.

The captain looked angry with everyone on the ship. We soon knew why. When we were in our cabin, he came in. 5

'Sir,' said the captain. 'I must tell you something. I don't like this journey. I don't like the men, and I don't like the first mate.' 10

'Perhaps you don't like the ship,' answered the squire. He was angry, too.

'I think she is a good ship,' said the captain.

'Then perhaps you don't like me,' shouted the squire. 15

Dr Livesey stopped them. 'Don't be angry,' he said. 'Captain, why don't you like this journey?'

'I don't like going on treasure journeys,' he said. 'It will be dangerous, and we may be killed.'

'I understand you,' said the doctor. 'You may be right. You said you don't like the crew. Are they not good sailors?'

'I just don't like them, sir,' said the captain.

The secret is known

'I have something to ask you,' the captain continued.
'First, the sailors are putting the guns and swords in
the front of the ship. You have a good place under
this cabin. Put them there. Second, your four servants
have their beds at the front of the ship. I want them
to sleep here, beside the cabin. One other thing.
Someone has talked about the secret.'

'Yes, we know who that was,' said the doctor,
looking at the squire.

'The men say that you have a map of an island,'
said the captain. 'They say there are crosses on the
map. The crosses show where the treasure is. They
also know where the island is.'

'I did not tell anyone that,' shouted the squire.

'I don't know who has the map,' said the captain.
'But you must not tell anyone where it is.'

'Captain,' said the doctor, 'are you afraid the sailors
will attack us?'

'I didn't say that,' said the captain. 'I think some of
the sailors are honest. They may all be good men.'

The voyage begins

Soon the men pulled the anchor up. The ship began
to move. The *Hispaniola* had begun her journey to
Treasure Island.

All the sailors liked Silver. He talked to them and
helped them. And the kitchen was always clean. He
had a parrot in the corner.

Long John was always kind to me. 'Come here,
Jim,' Silver said to me one day. 'Come and talk to me
and Captain Flint. Sit down here.'

I was surprised when he asked me to talk to Captain Flint.

'My parrot is called Captain Flint, you know,' he said. 'It has the same name as the famous pirate. Listen! Will we have a good journey, Captain Flint?' 5

'Pieces of eight! Pieces of eight!' was all that the parrot said. It couldn't say anything else.

'What are "pieces of eight"?' I asked.

'Money, Jim,' Silver replied. 'The kind that pirates keep in their treasure chests!'

We had some storms, but the *Hispaniola* was a very good ship. Almost everyone was happy. We were kind to the sailors. We gave them good food to eat and rum to drink.

The doctor told Silver to keep a barrel full of apples on the deck. The sailors could have an apple any time they felt hungry.

The captain said to the doctor, 'The men will not obey us if you are too kind.' But the doctor said the apples would stop the men becoming ill. The barrel was a good thing, too. It saved our lives. 25

Inside the barrel

It was in the sixth week of our journey to Treasure Island. We knew we were very close. The wind was good. Everyone was happy.

It was nearly dark, and I had finished my work. I 30 decided I wanted an apple. There were only a few. I had to climb into the barrel to reach one.

It was dark inside the barrel. Suddenly the barrel shook. Someone sat down next to it. I was going to jump out, but then I heard him speak. It was Silver's voice.

5 'No,' said Silver. 'Flint was the captain. Pew and I were on Flint's old ship together.'

'Flint was the best pirate,' said a younger voice.

'Yes, and we all became rich on Flint's ship.'

'Where is your money now?' asked the young 10 sailor.

'My wife has it,' said Silver.

'Well,' said the sailor, 'I don't like Captain Smollett, so I have decided I will work with you.'

'You will be a good pirate,' said Silver.

15 I knew, then, that Silver was a pirate.

Another man came and sat with them.

'Dick will work with us,' said Silver.

'Good. When will we be ready?' It was a sailor called Israel Hands.

20 'When we are very close to home,' Silver replied. 'Captain Smollett is a good captain. He sails the ship for us. The squire and the doctor have the map. They will find the treasure for us. They will help us put it on the ship.'

25 ## Silver's plan

'Captain Smollett will sail the ship part of the way home,' Silver continued. 'When we know the ship is going the right way, then we will be ready.'

'After we attack them, will we kill them?' asked 30 Dick.

'What do you think?' said Silver. 'Perhaps we will put them on an island. Or perhaps we will kill them. I don't know yet. Flint would have killed them.'

'Flint always said "Dead
men can't talk."' said Israel.
'You are right. I think we will kill them.
When I'm a rich man, I don't want to
meet Squire Trelawney on the street.'

'John,' said Israel, 'you're a clever man.'

'There is only one thing I want,' said Silver. 'I want
to kill Trelawney. Now, Dick! Get me an apple, will
you?'

An apple! I was in the apple barrel. They would   10
find me there. They would know I had heard every
word. They would kill me. I was very frightened. I
wanted to jump out and run.

I heard Dick stand up. Then someone started to
shout, 'Land! Land!'   15

People began to run onto the deck. I quickly
jumped out of the barrel.

TREASURE ISLAND

Silver sees a map

We could see land. Far away, in front of us, were two low hills. Behind one of them was a higher hill. I was glad to see the island, but I was still frightened of the pirates.

'Men,' said the captain, 'who has seen this land before?'

'I have,' said Silver. 'A ship I was on stopped to get water there once.'

'Is the harbour in the south, near a smaller island?' asked the captain.

'Yes, sir,' said Silver. 'The smaller one is called Skeleton Island. It was once a place for pirates. The three hills we can see are on Treasure Island. The one in the north is called Foremast Hill. The big one is called Spy-glass Hill.'

'I have a map here,' said Captain Smollett. 'Is this the place?'

Long John was excited to see the map. But the map was on a new piece of paper. This was not the treasure map. There were no red crosses or words on it.

Silver did not show that he was surprised, or angry. 'Yes, sir,' he said. 'This is the right place. This is a good map.'

'Thank you, Silver. That's all' said Captain Smollett. Silver walked away.

Captain Smollett's plans

The captain, the squire and Dr Livesey were talking together on the deck. Then they walked slowly down to the cabin. I waited for a few minutes, then I went to the cabin, too.   5

I told them all that Silver had said.

'Captain,' said the squire, 'you were right and I was wrong. I was very stupid.'

'These men are clever,' said the captain.

'Captain,' said the doctor, 'they all obey Silver.   10
Silver is the clever one.'

'I want Silver dead,' said the captain. 'We must decide what to do. I'll tell you my plans. First, we must continue, because we can't go back now. If we tried to go back to England, the men would attack   15
us. Second, we have time. They will not attack us until we find the treasure. Third, there are still some honest men. We will fight, but I think we must wait. Are your servants all honest men, Mr Trelawney?'

'Yes,' said the squire. 'And Jim can help us. The   20
men like him.'

I did not know how I could help. I was only a boy, not a man. But strange things happened later. Because of me, we got back to England safely.

There were twenty-six men on the ship. Only   25
seven were honest people, and I was one of the seven. So, six men and a boy were against nineteen bad men.

The *Hispaniola* drops anchor

The next morning we stopped in a little harbour   30
between the islands. Skeleton Island was on one side,

and Treasure Island was on the other. We could see the big hill. There was no wind.

The doctor smelled the air. He did not look happy. 'I don't know if there is treasure here, but I do know this is a bad place. The men will get ill here,' he said.

We went to the cabin. 'The men are unhappy. They will attack us,' said the captain. 'But perhaps Silver will help us. He wants the men to wait. The men will go on land in the afternoon. If they all go, we can take the ship. If none of them goes, we can get ready to fight them from the cabin. If some go, Silver will bring them back, but they will be happier.'

We decided to get ready. The captain gave us each a gun. We told Redruth, Joyce and Hunter about it, and gave them guns, too.

Then the captain went out. He told the sailors they could go on land. Silver said that six men must stay on the ship. The other thirteen could go on land with him.

Jim goes to the island

I decided to go on land, too. I wanted to see Treasure Island. I got into one of the little boats. One of the men saw me. 'Hide here, Jim,' he said. 'Then no-one will know where you are.'

Silver called out from another boat. He was looking for me. He was angry, and I was afraid of him.

Our boat arrived on the land. I got out quickly, ran into the woods and hid there.

After a while I heard voices. It was Silver and one of the other men. They were talking loudly. Silver wanted the man to join the pirates. The man said he would never do that. Suddenly Long John took out his sword. He hit the man with it. The man cried out loudly and fell down. He was dead.

I was very frightened. I ran and ran. I came to a place with no trees. There were small hills all around me. Only animals and birds lived there. I was happy to be alone and far away from Long John Silver.

I walked through the island until it was late. It began to grow dark. At last I came to a wood and a little river near the sea.

Then I saw something. It was running very quickly from tree to tree. It was like a man, but a very strange man. I remembered that I had my guns. I felt brave. I walked towards him.

Ben Gunn will help

The strange man knelt down in front of me. I looked at him.

'Who are you?' I asked.

'Ben Gunn,' he answered. 'I'm poor Ben Gunn. I have not talked to anyone for three years. What's your name?'

'Jim,' I told him.

His face was nice. His clothes were all old. 'What happened to you? Did your ship break on the rocks in a storm?' I asked.

'No, friend,' he said. 'Flint's men put me on this island and left me here. Now I live here. I live quite well. I eat goat's meat, and fruit, and fish. Perhaps you think I look poor, but I am rich. Let me help you, Jim. I will help you, and you will be rich, too.' Then he spoke in a low, quiet voice. 'Tell me, is that Flint's ship in the harbour?' he asked.

When I heard him say this, I knew he would help us.

I told him the story of our voyage and about the danger. When I had finished he said, 'Jim, you're a good boy. I will help you. Is the squire a kind man?'

I told him the squire was very kind, and would help him.

'Now,' I said, I must go back. How can I return to the ship?'

'I have a boat,' said Ben Gunn, 'I made it. It is under a white rock. We can go when it is dark. But what's that?'

We heard the noise of the ship's big gun. 'They are fighting!' I shouted. We began to run towards the harbour. Then, through the trees, I saw a flag flying. It was the British flag.

THE FIRST DAY'S FIGHTING

The doctor tells the story

The two boats left the *Hispaniola* and went to the island at one o'clock. The captain, the squire and I were in the cabin. We were talking.

Then Hunter came to tell us that Jim Hawkins had gone. He was on one of the boats. We knew Jim was honest. But we were afraid he would not be safe. We thought the men would kill him. We ran on deck.

The six men were talking on deck. We saw that the boats had reached the island. Most of the men had gone into the woods. One man was sitting in each boat.

We decided that Hunter and I would go to the island. There was one small boat left, and we would use that.

We went to the other side of the island. We could not see the ship from there, and no one could see us.

When we got to land I jumped out and began to walk. Soon I came to a small hill. At the top there was a wooden building with a fence all round it. It was a stockade.

The stockade

There was a spring of water at the top of the hill. Flint had built a strong wooden house here, many years ago. The house was big. There were special holes in the walls on every side. These were for guns.

Suddenly I heard a cry. It was the cry of a man who was dying. I ran to the boat. Quickly we rowed back to the *Hispaniola*.

All the people on the *Hispaniola* looked afraid.
5   They had heard the cry, too. The squire thought that the pirates had killed us.

The captain and I made a plan. We put guns, food, some brandy and my medicine box in the little boat. The captain called to Israel Hands. Hands was the
10 most important of the six sailors still on the boat.

'Mr Hands,' said the captain, 'the squire and I have two guns each. If anyone moves, we will kill him.'

The sailors were surprised. The squire made them go to the front of the ship.

15 Joyce, another sailor, and I got into the little boat. We rowed towards the island. The men who were on land saw us. I saw one of them run into the woods. He had gone to tell Silver.

We carried the things to the stockade. Joyce stayed
20 to watch. Hunter helped me carry more things from the boat. Then I rowed quickly back to the ship.

The ship's cannon

The squire was waiting for me. We took meat and biscuits and more guns and put them in the boat.
25 Redruth came and got into the boat too. Then Captain Smollett came.

The captain called to the six men in the front of the ship. 'Men,' he said, 'can you hear me?'

Nobody answered.

30 'Gray,' said Captain Smollett loudly, 'you must come with me. I know you are a good man.'

We heard men fighting. Then Gray ran towards the captain. A knife had cut his face. 'I'm with you,' he said.

Gray and the captain got into the boat with us. But we were not safe yet. We had to get to the stockade.   5

We began to row towards land. Suddenly, the captain spoke. 'Look!' he said. 'We forgot about the big cannon on the deck.' The five pirates were busy with it.

'Israel is good at shooting that cannon,' said Gray.   10

Trelawney tries to shoot Israel Hands

I could see and hear Israel Hands. He was telling the men to point the cannon at us.

'Which one of you can shoot well?' asked the captain.

'Mr Trelawney is the best,' I answered.

'Mr Trelawney, please shoot one of those men, sir. Try to shoot Israel Hands, if you can.'

We stopped rowing. Mr Trelawney lifted his gun. Israel Hands was standing behind the cannon. Trelawney fired. One of the four men behind Hands cried out loudly and fell.

5　We saw the men on the island looking at us. The pirates came out from the trees. They began to go to their boats. The men on the ship were ready to fire the cannon. They did not look at the man who was hurt. He was not dead.

10　'Ready!' shouted the squire.

'Row!' shouted the captain.

He and Redruth began to row the boat very fast. At the same time, we heard the gun from the ship. A heavy iron ball came flying towards us through the
15　air. It dropped into the sea. The ball made water come into our little boat. The boat sank but the sea was only a few feet deep there. We had arrived on the island.

We were lucky. No one was hurt. We walked to
20　the land. But most of our things were in the water. Only two of the guns were dry. The other guns were too wet to work.

Then we heard voices coming from the woods. We stopped thinking about the things in the boat, and
25　ran to the stockade.

Tom is hit

We ran through the woods. We could hear pirates' voices. Then we saw the stockade and ran faster. At the same time seven pirates ran out from the woods.
30　They stopped. They were surprised to see us. We fired our guns. One of them fell and died. The others ran away.

We were happy to get into the stockade. Then we heard the big gun. A cannon ball came flying across the trees. It hit Tom Redruth. He fell and I saw he was dying. We carried him into the stockade. He was a good man.

The squire knelt down and kissed his hand. He was crying. 'Tom,' he said, 'I'm sorry I brought you here.'

In a short time Redruth died. Later, the captain went on the roof, and put the British flag there.

We heard another cannon shot. The ball fell into the woods behind us.

All evening they were shooting the cannon at us. Most of the cannon balls fell outside the stockade.

Later, Gray and Hunter went to find the things that had fallen into the sea. But the pirates had already taken them. They saw Silver. He was back on the ship. He was telling the pirates what to do.

The pirates had taken the guns. Now every pirate had a gun and bullets.

We did not know where Jim was. We were afraid the pirates would hurt him. Then just before it got dark we heard someone shouting.

'Doctor! Squire! Captain! Hunter!' the voice called. Then I saw Jim Hawkins climbing over the stockade fence.

THE PIRATES ATTACK

Jim tells the story again

When Ben Gunn saw the flag, he stopped. 'There are your friends,' he said. 'They're in the stockade. Flint made that stockade many years ago.'

5   'Well,' I said, 'We must join them.'

'You go alone,' Ben said. 'When they want me, Jim, I will be where you found me today. The man who comes must carry something white in his hand. He must come alone. Tell them I have something to say

10 to them. I want to see the squire or the doctor. If you see Silver, don't tell him about me. He must not know that I am here.'

I said I would do what he asked. Then the guns became very loud. A cannon ball came very close.

15 Ben ran into the wood. I ran to the stockade.

At the stockade, we ate our food, and had some wine to drink. After dinner, the three leaders talked. I slept.

The next morning, when I woke up I heard a loud

20 voice calling. It was Silver.

'What do you want?' the captain shouted.

'Don't shoot!' Long John answered.

'I don't want to talk to you,' said Captain Smollett. 'But if you want to talk to me you can come in. We

25 won't hurt you.'

Silver came to the door.

'What do you want, Silver?' said the captain.

The pirates want the map

'You killed one of my men last night. I was sleeping. If I had been awake I would have killed you.'

The captain did not understand, but Silver did not know this. I thought perhaps Ben Gunn had killed one of them.

'We want the treasure,' Silver continued. 'You have a map. You give us the treasure map, and stop killing my men when they are asleep. And we will give you your lives. After we have the treasure, you can come on the ship. We will take you to a safe place. Or you can stay here and we will give you some of the treasure.'

Captain Smollett stood up. 'Is that all you want to say?' he asked.

'Yes,' answered Silver. 'If you say no, we will only send you some more cannon balls.'

'Silver,' said the captain, 'you can't find the treasure. You can't sail the ship. You can't fight us. You can't escape. If you want, I will take you to England, all your men, without your guns. There I will give you to the police. If you say no, the next time I meet you I will kill you. Now, go away from here quickly.'

Silver went away. He was angry.

The attack begins

'Men,' said the captain, 'Silver is angry. Soon, they will attack us and they have more men than we have. We must get ready to fight.'

On the east and west walls of the house there were two holes. On the south, there were two holes. On the north, there were five. There were twenty guns for the seven of us.

'Doctor, you will go to the door,' said the captain.
'Hunter, go to the east side. Joyce, you go to the west
side. Mr Trelawney, you and Gray go to the north
side. That will be the most dangerous side. Jim, you
5 and I will help the others.'

After an hour, the firing began on all the sides.
Some bullets hit the house, but not one came in.
Then it was quiet.

'Did you kill one of them?' the captain asked Joyce.
10 'No, I don't think so,' Joyce answered.

Suddenly, we heard a loud shout. Some pirates
came from the woods on the north side. They ran
towards the wooden fence. The others began to
shoot from the woods. A bullet came through the
15 door and broke the doctor's gun.

Over the fence

The pirates climbed over the stockade fence. The
squire and Gray fired again and again. Three men
fell.

20 Four men were inside the fence. They ran towards
the house. I saw the face of a pirate called Job
Anderson. He was looking through one of the holes.
'Kill them all!' he shouted.

Another pirate pulled Hunter's gun away from him.
25 He hit Hunter with it. Hunter fell. Another attacked
the doctor with his sword.

I took a sword. Then I ran outside. Someone was
behind me. In front, the doctor was fighting a pirate.
The pirate fell. Then the doctor cut the man's face.
30 Suddenly I saw Job Anderson in front of me. He shouted
loudly and lifted his sword. I saw the sword coming
towards me. I jumped to one side and fell down.

When I stood up, I saw
the other pirates climbing
back over the stockade fence.
One man was on top of the fence.
Gray was behind me. He had killed Job Anderson.   5
The doctor had killed another man with his sword.

The doctor shouted, 'You men can go back inside
the house now.' The other pirates had all run away.

The doctor, Gray and I ran back to the house. We
thought that the pirates would soon return. They   10
would start shooting at us. Joyce was dead. In the
centre of the room, the squire was holding the
captain.

'The captain is hurt,' said Squire Trelawney.

'Did they run away?' asked the captain.   15

'Yes,' answered the doctor. 'But five of them are
dead.'

'Five!' said the captain. 'That is good. Four of us
against nine of them, now.'

8

BACK ON THE *HISPANIOLA*

Jim runs away

The pirates did not return. They did not shoot at us
again. After dinner, the squire and the doctor sat with
the captain to talk. When they had finished, the
doctor stood up. He took his guns and swords. He
put the treasure map in his pocket, and walked out.

'Why is the doctor going out?' Gray asked.

'I think he wants to see Ben Gunn,' I said.

I was right.

We waited. I began to think the house was very
hot. There were too many dead people around me.
I hated being there. I wanted to run away. I put some
biscuits in my pocket. I took two guns. I thought I
would go to the sea, and find the white rock. I
wanted to find Ben Gunn's boat.

The squire and Gray were busy helping the
captain. No one was watching me. I ran outside and
into the trees.

I found Ben Gunn's boat. It was a strange boat,
and not a very good one. But it was very light and
I could carry it easily.

I decided to row to the *Hispaniola* and cut the
anchor rope. Most of the pirates were on the island.
I knew they wanted to sail away. I wanted to stop
them.

When it was dark I carried the boat to the water.
I was lucky. The sea water was going out. It carried
my little boat to the *Hispaniola*.

Cutting the anchor rope

The waves were strong now. Soon, I was holding the anchor rope. A few cuts, and the *Hispaniola* would sail away on the waves.

I cut the rope. The ship began to move slowly. Then I saw another, thinner rope. It was at the side of the *Hispaniola,* near the back of the ship. I wanted to see inside the ship's cabin. I took hold of the rope. I pulled and pulled. When the little boat was near the window, I stood up in it. I could see into the cabin.

I saw Israel Hands and another man. They were fighting. I quickly sat down again, and looked towards the land. Behind me I saw a fire. The pirates had lit it on the beach. I was frightened.   20

Suddenly, the *Hispaniola* moved. I heard someone shouting. I heard them running on to the deck. I sat down in Ben Gunn's little boat, so they could not see me. There was nothing they could do. There were only two men on the ship. All the little boats were   25
on the island.

I was out at sea in Ben Gunn's boat for many hours. Soon I grew very tired. I slept and dreamed of home and the Admiral Benbow.

When I woke up it was light. I saw I was near the   30
south end of Treasure Island. I was very close to the shore. At first I thought I would row my little boat to land. Then I saw the *Hispaniola* very close to me.

I thought the pirates would see me and take me prisoner. But I looked at the ship and saw that it was not moving.

'Perhaps the sailors are drunk again,' I thought.

The ship sailed towards me for a minute and then stopped. This happened many times. The ship went north, south, west and east. But it always stopped before it had gone very far.

'Where are the sailors?' I thought. 'If I can get on the ship, I could take it to the captain.' I was excited. I was also thirsty. I knew there was water on the ship, so I became very brave.

Going on the *Hispaniola*

I began to row towards the *Hispaniola*. I could not see anyone on the deck. The *Hispaniola* was not moving. I was almost there.

Then, suddenly, the wind blew. I had no time to think. The ship came towards me very quickly. As the ship went past I took hold of one of the ropes. I jumped. There was a noise. The *Hispaniola* hit my little boat, and it went under water. Now, there was no way for me to return to the island, but I was alive!

I climbed up the rope onto the deck. The deck was dirty. Everywhere there were empty rum bottles. Then I saw the two seamen. One was lying on his back. His mouth was open. Israel Hands was lying there too.

His head was against the side of the ship. His face was very white. I saw red blood on the deck around them. I thought they had killed each other.

While I was looking at them, Israel Hands moved his head. He made a sound. He was very weak and in great pain. But I remembered he was a bad man. I walked towards him and spoke to him. He said only one word, 'Brandy'.

I knew he would soon die. I ran to the cabin. I found a bottle of brandy. I took it to Hands.

I sat in a corner. 'Are you hurt?' I asked.

'Yes.'

'I am the captain, now, Hands.'

He looked angry, but said nothing.

'Hands,' I said, 'I don't like that black pirate flag. I will take it down.'

I pulled down the ugly flag and threw it into the sea. 'Now, the ship is ours again, not the pirates'.'

'I think, Captain Jim, you want to go to land now,' Hands said.

'Yes,' I replied, 'I do.'

'You can't sail her alone. I will help you. I will tell you what to do. You give me food and drink, and I will tell you how to sail her. All right?'

We decided to help each other. We began sailing to the North Inlet. It was a sunny day, with a good wind. We had water to drink and food to eat. I knew the others would be happy that I had the ship again.

But Israel Hands was watching me. He watched and watched me, while I worked. There was a strange smile on his face. It was an evil smile.

ISRAEL HANDS

Sailing the *Hispaniola*

'Jim,' said Israel, 'go to the cabin and bring me some wine.'

I knew he wanted me to go away, but I didn't
know why. I answered him quickly. 'Yes, I will go.'

I ran down the stairs. Then I quietly went up the other stairs to watch him.

I saw him move quickly across the deck. He picked up a sword that was lying on the deck. The sword
had blood on it. He hid it near where he was sitting.

I knew he wanted to kill me.

I found the wine and went back on deck. Hands sat there as if he had not moved. He looked up when I came to him. He took the bottle.

'Now, Jim,' he said, 'we'll sail the ship to the island.'

We began to sail into the North Inlet. 'Look, there,' said Hands. 'There is a good place. Flat sand with trees around it.' He gave the orders. I held the tiller. Then suddenly he cried, 'To the wind!'

I moved the *Hispaniola* quickly. We were sailing towards the land.

Israel Hands attacks

I was excited and I forgot to watch Hands. I stood looking, waiting to reach land. Suddenly, I heard a
noise behind me. I looked. Israel Hands was standing there. He had the sword in his right hand.

I was very frightened. He jumped towards me, and I jumped to the side. I forgot about the tiller. It saved my life. The tiller hit Hands and knocked him down.

I ran across the deck. I tried to fire my guns, but they did not work. Hands was hurt, but he could still move very fast.

Suddenly, the *Hispaniola* hit the land. We both fell over. I stood up first. I ran to the ship's mast and climbed up.

Hands threw a knife at me, but it did not hit me. He stood on the deck and looked up. He looked surprised.

Now I had time to put bullets in my guns. Hands was afraid. He began to climb up to me. He held another knife in his teeth. He came up slowly.

'If you come up here, I'll kill you,' I said.

He stopped.

'Jim,' he said, 'you win.'

I smiled. But suddenly, I saw his right hand move. He threw his knife. I was surprised. I fired both my guns. Israel screamed and fell into the water. I knew he was dead.

The knife hit my leg. I pulled it out. There was a lot of blood and my leg hurt very much.

A fire

I decided to walk across the island to the stockade.
It grew very dark. After a long time, I saw the
wooden house. On one side there was a big fire. No
5   one was moving. I could not hear anything.

I walked quietly to the side of the stockade. I
reached the door of the house and looked in. I could
not see anything. It was dark inside. I could hear men
sleeping.

10   Suddenly, a high voice called out. 'Pieces of eight!
Pieces of eight! Pieces of eight!' It was Captain Flint,
Silver's green parrot.

I had no time to run away. The men all woke up.
'Who is that?' someone shouted. It was Silver.

15   I ran, but I ran into someone. He held my arm.
'Bring me a light, Dick,' said Silver. One of the men
went out and brought in a light from the fire.

I could see the inside of the house. The pirates
were living there. There were six of them. The others
20   were all dead.

'So, here is Jim Hawkins,' said Silver. 'He has come
to visit us. That is nice.' Silver sat down.

'Jim,' he said, 'I'll tell you what I think. I like you.
You are a brave boy. I want you to join us. The doctor
25   and the captain are very angry with you. You can't
return to them. They won't take you back. If you
don't join us you will be alone.'

I did not believe him. I knew the others would be
angry, but I was very glad to know they were alive.

30   'Well,' I said, 'where are my friends now, and why
are you here?'

Silver spoke kindly to me, 'Yesterday morning,
Doctor Livesey came to see us. He held a white flag.

"Silver," he said, "the ship is not here." We looked at the harbour. It was true. The ship was not there. So we made a bargain. We took the house, the goods, the brandy, and the wood. The others walked away. I don't know where they are.'

5

Jim will help

I looked at Silver. 'Let me tell you something,' I said. 'You have lost the ship, you do not know where the treasure is, most of your men are dead. If you want to know why, it was because of me. I was in the apple barrel on the night we saw land. I heard you talking, John Silver. I told the others everything you said. I cut the ship's anchor rope, too. And I killed the men on the ship. Now you can kill me, if you like. But if you don't, I will try to help you.'

10

15

No one moved. 'Mr Silver,' I said, 'if you kill me, tell the doctor I tried to be brave.'

'I will remember to do that,' said Silver, quietly.

'Jim knew Black Dog,' shouted Morgan.

'Yes, I believe Jim did know him,' said Silver. 'And I believe Jim did do all those things.'

20

'Then I will kill him,' said Morgan. He jumped up, and pulled out his knife.

'Stop!' shouted Silver. Morgan stopped.

The other men were angry with Silver. 'Who wants to fight me?' shouted Silver. 'If you try to kill Jim, I will kill you!'

Nobody moved. Not one man answered.

Silver saves Jim

'Jim is a good boy,' said Silver. 'He is braver than all of you. You must not hurt him. Do you understand?'

No one answered. I stood against a wall. I was still very frightened. Silver was watching his men. They began to whisper to each other.

'Sir,' said one of the men, 'I know you are the captain, but we are not happy. We want to talk alone, outside.'

The men walked out of the house.

'Listen, Jim,' said Silver to me, 'they want to kill you. They are going to choose another captain. I am going to help you. I will save your life. You must save my life in London.'

'You mean that you know you have lost everything?' I asked.

'Yes, I do,' he answered. 'The ship is lost and I can't do anything without it. I will save your life if I can. But you must help me, too. You must save me from being punished.'

'I will try,' I said.

'I'm on the squire's side now, Jim. I know that the ship is safe somewhere. I don't know how you did it. But there is something I do not understand. Why did the doctor give me the map, Jim?'

I was very surprised.

THE BLACK MARK

'I don't want to be your captain'

The door opened. The five men stood there. 'What do you want?' said Silver. A pirate came forward. He put something in Silver's hand. Silver looked at it. It was a small piece of paper.

'The black mark!' he said.

'Read the other side,' said one of the men.

'Thank you, George,' said Silver and he looked at the other side. ' "You are not the captain now," ' he read out. 'Did you write this, George? Are you the new captain?'

Silver threw a piece of paper on the floor. I knew what it was. It was the treasure map.

When the men saw the map, they were very happy. They fought to pick it up. Then they all looked at it.

'Yes,' said one man, 'this is Flint's map.'

'Very good,' said George, 'but how are we going to take the treasure away, Silver? We have no ship.'

'Don't ask me,' Silver shouted. 'You tell me. You and the others lost the ship because you are stupid. You lost the ship and I found the treasure. Which was better? And now I don't want to be your captain!'

'We want Silver for captain!' all the pirates shouted.

'And this black mark?' Silver threw it to me. 'Here, Jim, you can keep it,' he said. I still have that terrible piece of paper.

'A good and honest man'

In the morning, a shout woke me. 'Hello!' someone called.

'It's the doctor,' said George.

5   'Good morning to you,' shouted Silver. He was awake and smiling. 'A young friend of yours is here with us.'

Dr Livesey said, 'Not Jim!'

'Yes, Jim!' said Silver.

10   The doctor stood still and did not speak. Then he said, 'First, I will look at the men who are ill.'

The doctor gave them all medicine. Then he spoke again. 'And now, I want to talk to that boy, please.'

Silver looked hard at all the men. 'Doctor,' he said, 15 'I know you like Jim. You are kind to us, and give us medicine. You can talk to Jim if he says he will not run away.'

I said, 'I will not run away.'

'Doctor,' said Silver, 'you go outside the stockade. 20 When you are there, I will bring the boy. He can stay on the inside, and you can talk to him. Goodbye, sir.'

A few minutes later we walked very slowly towards the doctor. When we were close, Silver stopped. 'Remember that I'm helping you now, doctor,' he 25 said. 'Jim will tell you how I saved his life. It is dangerous for me to help you.' Silver looked afraid.

'John, are you afraid?' asked Dr Livesey.

'Doctor,' answered Silver, 'I am afraid of being punished. You are a good and honest man. I know 30 you will remember the bad things I have done. But I also know you will not forget the good things I did.' Silver walked away.

Jim tells about the ship

'Jim,' said the doctor sadly, 'you ran away when Captain Smollett was ill. It was a bad thing to do.'

I began to cry. 'Doctor,' I said, 'please do not be angry with me. I am going to be killed. I would be dead now if Silver had not helped me. I am afraid.'

'Jim,' the doctor stopped me. 'Jim, jump over the wall, and we'll run away.'

'Doctor, I told Silver I would not run away. Silver believed me. I must go back. But, Doctor, I have something to tell you. I took the ship. The ship is in the North Inlet on the south beach.'

'The ship!' said the doctor, surprised.

I quickly told him my story.

'You have saved our lives, Jim,' said the doctor. 'You have helped us many times. You discovered the pirates on the ship. You found Ben Gunn. Now you have got the ship back for us.'

Silver came back. 'We must go and find the treasure,' he said. 'Then we can save my life and Jim's.'

'Well, Silver,' answered the doctor. 'When you find it, be careful. Call us if you need help.'

The hunt begins

The doctor went away. Soon afterwards we left the stockade. We looked very strange. The sailors' clothes were dirty. Each man carried knives and guns. I had a rope around me. Silver held the end of it. I had to follow him. We went to the two boats on the beach.

The men talked about the map. The words on the back said:

'Tall tree. Spy-glass to the N of NNE. Skeleton Island ESE by E. Ten feet.'

First we had to find the place, and then we had to
find the tree.

We went to the mouth of the river on the side of
Spy-glass Hill. Then
5   we began to climb.
We walked half
a mile. We had
almost reached
the top when
10 one of the men
began to shout.
The others ran
towards him.

The man had
15 found a skeleton
with old clothes
on it. The skeleton
was lying close
to a big tree.
20 Everyone was
frightened.

'He was a sailor,' said George. 'These are sailors'
clothes.'

'Yes,' said Silver. 'He was. But, look, the skeleton's
25 feet are pointing one way and his hands are pointing
the other. They are above his head. Here is a
compass. See which way the bones are pointing.'

The body pointed to Skeleton Island, ESE by E.

'This skeleton is showing us which way to go,' said
30 Silver. 'Flint did this. He had six men with him here.
He killed them. This is one of them. Come, we must
find the gold.'

We went. The pirates did not run now. They had
seen the dead sailor. Now *they* were afraid.

THE TREASURE HUNT

Ghosts

We sat down at the top of the hill. Silver looked at his compass.

'There are three tall trees,' he said. 'And I think Spy-glass is that hill over there. It will be easy to find the gold now.'

Suddenly, far away, a high voice began to sing,
> *'Fifteen men on the Dead Man's Chest*
> *'Yo-ho-ho and a bottle of rum!'*

The pirates' faces went white. Some of them jumped up.

'It's Flint,' said Merry.

The song stopped suddenly.

'I wasn't afraid of Flint when he was alive. I am not afraid of him dead,' said Silver. But the others were very frightened.

'Don't talk like that, John,' said Merry. 'The ghost will be angry.'

'I think we made a mistake,' said George. 'It was like Flint's voice, but it wasn't the same. It was more like ...'

'I know,' said Silver. 'That was Ben Gunn's voice!'

'Yes, it was,' shouted Morgan. 'It was Ben Gunn!'

'But Ben Gunn is dead, too,' said Dick.

'Perhaps he is. But nobody is afraid of Ben Gunn, dead or alive,' answered Merry.

The men laughed. Suddenly they were very happy. Soon, they were talking again. They picked up their things and we continued walking.

We reached the first tall tree. It was in the wrong place. So was the second. The third tree was very, very tall. Silver walked fast. He was excited.

The gold is not there

5 We arrived at the foot of the tree. 'Come, friends,' shouted Merry. The others began to run.

Suddenly, they stopped. They began to speak angrily to each other. Silver walked more quickly. The next minute, he and I stopped, too.

10 In front of us was a large hole. It was not a new hole. There was grass at the bottom. Someone had found the gold and taken it away. They had taken it away a long time ago.

The men were very surprised. They could not
15 believe it. Silver thought quickly. He was not angry. 'Jim,' he said quietly, 'take this gun and be ready for something bad to happen.'

The pirates were shouting. They jumped into the hole,
20 and began to dig with their fingers. Morgan found a piece of gold. He held it up and  showed it to the others. It was a two-guinea coin.

'Two guineas!' shouted Morgan. 'Is this your
25 treasure, Silver? You stupid sailor!'

The pirates climbed out of the hole. We stood there. Silver and I were on one side. The five men were on the other side. No one moved.

Merry said, 'Friends, there are only two of them
30 there. One has a wooden leg. He brought us here. The other is a boy who has given us a lot of trouble. I am going to kill that boy first.'

He was going to shoot. Then there was the sound
of three guns firing from the woods. Merry fell into
the hole. Another man fell on his side. The other
three ran away into the woods.

The doctor, Gray, and Ben Gunn came out of the
trees.

Ben Gunn's place

As we walked back to the boats, the doctor told us
their story.

Ben had found the skeleton and the treasure when
he was alone on the island. He had carried the
treasure to the cave where he lived.

Ben Gunn told the doctor about this on the
afternoon of the attack. The next morning, the doctor
saw the ship had gone. He went to Silver and gave
him the treasure map and the goods. Then they all
moved to Ben Gunn's cave. Ben Gunn had a lot food
there. And they could watch the treasure there, too.

Then, that morning, the doctor had found me with
the pirates. He knew they would take me with them
to look for the treasure. He decided that the squire
should stay with the captain, who was still ill. Gray
and Ben Gunn went with the doctor to the old
treasure hole. Ben Gunn got there first. When Ben
Gunn saw us coming he decided to be Flint's ghost.

'I was lucky Jim was with me,' said Silver. 'You
would have killed me.'

'That is right,' said the doctor.

The treasure

Outside Ben's cave, the squire met us. He was kind
to me. Then he saw Silver.

'John Silver,' he said, 'you are an evil and bad man.
I was told not to punish you. Well, I will not. But
many men are dead because of you!'

'Thank you, sir,' Long John said.

5   'Don't thank me,' shouted the squire.
'I want to kill you!'

Then we all went into Ben Gunn's
cave. It was large. There was a
little spring inside with clear

10 water. The floor was sand.
Captain Smollett was in
front of a big fire. I
saw the gold — the
treasure — in the

15 corner. Seventeen
men died because
of it.

The next morning we began work early. The gold
had to be carried a mile to the beach. Then it went

20 by boat to the *Hispaniola*. We were busy all day. We
worked many days carrying the gold to the ship. It
was very heavy.

One night, Dr Livesey and I went out walking.
Suddenly we heard a noise. Some men were singing.

25 'It is the pirates!' said the doctor.

'They are all drunk,' said Silver.

But we did not see them. They did not trouble us
as we took the gold to the ship. Once we heard the
sound of a gun. It was a long way away. We thought

30 they were hunting for food.

THE END OF MY STORY

Leaving Treasure Island

We decided we would not take the three pirates home with us. We would leave them on the island. Ben Gunn was very happy when he heard this. But we left some food and medicine for them, and also some rope, an old sail, and some bullets for their guns. They would be able to live quite well. *5*

One sunny morning we pulled up the anchor and our voyage back to England began. We put up the British flag. The *Hispaniola* began to move. As we sailed out of the North Inlet, we went quite close to the shore. *10*

The three pirates were waiting for us on the beach there. They were kneeling on the sand. They held their arms out to us, and called to us. They wanted us to take them with them. *15*

We felt very sad. But if we took them it would be dangerous for us. It would be dangerous for them, too. When they got back to England they would be punished and killed. *20*

The doctor shouted to them. He told them where to find the things we had left for them.

When they saw we would not stop they shouted to us more and more loudly. Then one of them jumped up. He had a gun. He fired it at Silver. *25*

Silver was lucky. The bullet went flying over his head. It made a small hole in the sail. We all got down by the side of the deck to keep safe.

When I next looked, the pirates had gone. The shores of Treasure Island were moving slowly away from us. Before midday we could see nothing of the island any more, and I was very happy.

South America

There were only seven of us. The captain was still too weak to work. Silver could not work very well with his wooden leg, and I was only a boy. It was difficult to sail the *Hispaniola* with so few men. We all worked very hard, and we all got very tired.

We sailed to the nearest harbour to get some more men. It was in South America.

The doctor and the squire went on to the land. They took me with them. We went to see the town, and to look for men to sail the *Hispaniola*.

Here we met the captain of a large English ship. He took us to his ship and gave us a good dinner there. When we returned to the *Hispaniola* it was nearly morning.

Silver leaves us

We found Ben Gunn standing alone on the deck. He looked very excited.

'Silver has gone,' he said. 'I saw him take a little boat and row away.'

'You should have tried to stop him,' the squire said.

But Ben Gunn had not tried to stop him. He told us he was sure that if Silver sailed with us to England he would kill us all.

We went down to our cabin. Some of the treasure had gone. Silver had cut a hole in the wall and taken one of the bags of gold.

I think we were all happy that he had gone. The gold he had taken was not important. There was plenty of treasure left for us.

The next day we soon found some good men to help us sail the ship. We returned to England safely. 10

We were happy to get home, but sad as well. Of all the men who had sailed away from Bristol in the *Hispaniola*, only five of us came back. Almost all the others were dead.

We all took a large part of the treasure. Most of us 15 did good things with the money.

Captain Smollett does not work at sea any more. Gray used his money to study. He now has his own ship. He is married and has a family. Ben Gunn received a thousand pounds. He spent it all in 20 nineteen days. On the twentieth day he started begging. We gave him a small house in the country. He lives there and sings in the church on Sundays. All the people like him.

I do not know where Silver is now. Perhaps he is 25 living happily with his wife and Captain Flint, the parrot, in South America.

I am sure there is a lot more of Flint's treasure somewhere on the island, but I will never go back there. I hate the place. Sometimes, late at night, I still 30 hear the noise of the waves breaking on those dark shores. I dream about Silver's parrot. I suddenly sit up in bed, frightened, and hear it shouting: 'Pieces of eight! Pieces of eight!'

QUESTIONS AND ACTIVITIES

CHAPTER 1

Put these sentences in the right order; the first one is correct.

1 One day an old seaman came to stay at the inn.
2 Then a blind man put something in the Captain's hand.
3 Jim and his parents called him 'the Captain'.
4 Soon after that, the Captain died.
5 He asked to see the Captain, and they had a fight.
6 Later, a rough seaman called Black Dog came.

CHAPTER 2

Use these words to fill the gaps: ***island, cloth, map, chest, crosses, papers, treasure.***

Jim showed Dr Livesey and Squire Trelawney a (1) _____ bag he had found in the Captain's (2) _____. The doctor took some (3) _____ from the bag. One of them was a (4) _____ of an (5) _____. There were three red (6) _____ on it. One showed where the (7) _____ was.

CHAPTER 3

Choose the right words to fill the gaps.

Long John Silver went with Jim to the (1) **house/inn** where the squire was staying. On the way he told (2) **Black Dog/Jim** many interesting things about (3) **ships/the land** and the sea. Silver told the squire about (4) **Black Dog/Billy Bones**. The squire thanked (5) **Jim/Silver** for trying to help. The squire and (6) **Hunter/Dr Livesey** both thought Silver was a (7) **good/bad** man.

CHAPTER 4

*Who said or did these things? Choose from **Silver**, **Dick** and **Israel Hands**. Some names must be used more than once.*

Jim was in the apple barrel. He could hear Silver, Dick and Israel Hands talking. (1) _____ said he did not like Captain Smollett, and he wanted to work with the pirates. (2) _____ asked when they would be ready. (3) _____ said they would be ready when they were close to home. (4) _____ asked if they would kill the Captain, the squire and the doctor. (5) _____ said he wanted to kill the squire.

CHAPTER 5

Put the letters of these words in the right order. The first one is 'sailors'.

Captain Smollett said the (1) **rassoli** could leave the ship and go to the (2) **snidal**. Jim wanted to see Treasure Island, so he hid in one of the little (3) **sobat**. When they got to the island, Jim went into the (4) **oswod** by himself. Then he heard Silver and (5) **trohane** man talking. He watched them. Silver took out his sword and (6) **leklid** the man. Jim was very (7) **fendigther** and ran away.

CHAPTER 6

Something is wrong in the underlined part of each sentence. What should it be?

1 The Captain and Dr Livesey <u>put some money, guns and the doctor's medicine bag</u> into the little boat.
2 The Captain and the squire <u>made the sailors stand at the back of the *Hispaniola*</u>.
3 <u>Then the Captain, Joyce and Hunter rowed to the island</u> and took the things to the stockade.
4 Dr Livesey and Hunter <u>left Joyce in the woods to watch their things</u>, and rowed back to the Hispaniola.
5 Then the Captain, the squire, and Gray <u>got into the boat and went to the stockade with Dr Livesey and Joyce</u>.

CHAPTER 7

Put the endings in the correct boxes.

1 Silver said that he wanted the Captain to …	(a) fire some more cannon balls.
2 He said that he would let the Captain and his friends …	(b) give him the treasure map.
3 If the Captain did not agree, the pirates would …	(c) come on the ship.

CHAPTER 8

Put the words at the end of each sentence in the right order.

1 Jim got Ben Gunn's boat   [the] [rowed] [and] [*Hispaniola*] [to].

2 He cut the rope, and the   [began] [to] [away] [ship] [sail].

3 In the morning   [the] [Jim] [onto] [climbed] [ship].

4 He found Israel Hands   [the] [lying] [on] [deck] [ship's].

5 Jim said he   [would] [captain] [be] [the].

CHAPTER 9

Some of these sentences are true and some are false. Which ones are true? What is wrong with the false ones?

1 Jim walked across the island to the *Hispaniola*.
2 When he arrived, one of Silver's men cried out.
3 Jim found that the pirates were living in the stockade.
4 A pirate called Morgan wanted to kill Silver.
5 Silver told Jim that he would give him some money.
6 He said Jim must help him when they got to London.

CHAPTER 10

Copy the table and put the missing words in the right places.
Choose from: **pirates, clothes, stretched, rope, skeleton, sailors, stockade, Flint, treasure.**

Silver, the other men and Jim left the (1) _____ to look for the (2) _____. Jim had a (3) _____ round him, and Silver held one end of it. The (4) _____ were afraid when they saw a (5) _____. It had some old (6) _____ on it. Silver said that this had once been one of (7) _____'s (8) _____. The arms were (9) _____ out one way, and the legs another.

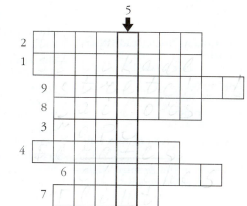

CHAPTER 11

Put these sentences in the right order; the first one is correct.

1 When they reached the third tree, Silver became excited.
2 They were going to kill Silver and Jim.
3 The other pirates began to run ahead.
4 The pirates were very angry and took out their guns.
5 Then they stopped at the side of a large, empty hole.

CHAPTER 12

Choose the right words.

Jim and his friends left Treasure Island. They sailed to the nearest (1) **harbour/island** to get more men. When they were on another ship there, (2) **Silver/Ben Gunn** took a bag of (3) **food/gold**, and ran away. They found some good men and returned to (4) **South America/England** safely.